The Opposite of Cabbage

ROB A. MACKENZIE was born in Glasgow. He studied law and then abandoned the possibility of significant personal wealth by switching to theology. He spent a year in Seoul, eight years in Lanarkshire, five years in Turin, and now lives in Edinburgh where he organises the Poetry at the Great Grog reading series. His pamphlet collection, *The Clown of Natural Sorrow*, was published by HappenStance Press in 2005 and he blogs at Surroundings (http://robmack.blogspot.com).

Also by Rob A. Mackenzie

POETRY CHAPBOOK
The Clown of Natural Sorrow (HappenStance, 2005)

The Opposite of Cabbage

ROB A. MACKENZIE

SALT

CAMBRIDGE

PUBLISHED BY SALT PUBLISHING
14a High Street, Fulbourn, Cambridge CB21 5DH United Kingdom

© Rob A. Mackenzie, 2009, 2010

The right of Rob A. Mackenzie to be identified as the
author of this work has been asserted by him in accordance
with Section 77 of the Copyright, Designs and Patents Act 1988.

Salt Publishing 2009
Paperback edition 2010

Printed and bound in the United Kingdom by Lightning Source UK Ltd

Typeset in Swift 9.5 / 13

ISBN 978 1 84471 513 8 hardback
ISBN 978 1 84471 774 3 paperback

1 3 5 7 9 8 6 4 2

to Anne and Alyssa

Contents

Acknowledgements

Some of these poems appeared in the following magazines and anthologies: *Anon, Chapman, Fourteen, Horizon Review* (http://www.saltpublishing.com/horizon), *Magma, Mimesis, New Writing 15, Pushing Out the Boat, Read This!, Rising, Seam* and *Succour.*

'In the Last Few Seconds' was commended in the National Poetry Competition 2005.

An earlier version of 'Hangover Hotel' was highly commended in the Poetry on the Lake Competition 2007.

Three poems in this collection first appeared in the pamphlet collection, *The Clown of Natural Sorrow* (HappenStance, 2005).

'Advice from the Lion-Tamer to the Poetry Critic' featured in the pamphlet anthology, *Unsuitable Companions* (HappenStance, 2007)

My thanks are extended to A. B. Jackson, Andrew Philip, Helena Nelson, James Midgley, and Nicolette Bethel for their support, and for intelligent criticism on many of the poems in this collection.

Stephen Burt's use of 'Ashbery' as an end-word in his fine sestina, 'Six Kinds of Noodles', was the inspiration behind 'A Creative Writing Tutor Addresses his Star Pupil.'

The Opposite of Cabbage

Light Storms from a Dark Country

You bend sleetward down grey alleyways,
    in search of finesse to straighten out
the tangle of the last spat. The sky's
    watery glaze reminds you of that night
you split. A shock of white chrysanthemums
    droops from an abandoned briefcase
on the kerb. They shatter in the slipstream
    of a truck. You count the Christmas trees
that line the tinselled storefront. They flicker
    pink, blue and saffron like a funeral
in Hollywood. You search for living flowers,
    as a peace offering, but when you steal
the twisted stems dumped at the cenotaph
    days before, you know it must be over.
Freak lightning tears its jack-knife
    through the sky. You swerve under cover
with other hunched men, all asking what
    flares in love, why it turns to smoke,
why by any other slant of light
    you never move forward, never back.

Voices

We staggered down the via della Guerra, the wind
snatching at the bedlam of each overflowing bin,
and you told me of voices crowding your head
like sharp stones, as if the entire street had moved in
with simultaneous post-theatre analysis, girls on boys
and boys on girls, drunk sermons on the brink
of violence, and how often the confusion
made more sense than a single, real voice,
including mine—a gloss which left me speechless
as we entered the bar and your beer order
was understood despite the anarchy
of discourse drifting to the ceiling fan,
which is where most conversations drift
and spin at a height and resonance
just beyond reach, along the wiry ventricles
of the city's brain, before settling
for that rented room where my reply, finally
and dutifully performed, is already dulling
to a murmur beneath the bed's bright quilt.

The Listeners

The thrill of the fair is not in the glamorous machinery
and its spin, or in the clamour of infants longing
to be heard, but in the hour when music stops
and lights blink out, when a man threads a dark path
among greyer darknesses of once-bright carousels,
and becomes, with them, a bearer of absence,
night's counterpart, impossible to bring to focus.

The stars have plucked their eyes from the world,
which has become a mirror of blindness, blind
also to itself. Only the man's uncertain steps alert
his listeners to its presence. So when they screw
open a cheap Cabernet and lose track halfway
through his walk from Waltzer to Big Wheel
and dawn spills out like an over-familiar friend,
they feel grief that the night is unrepeatable
as its secrets, as footsteps that leave no echo.

White Noise

From a third floor window, low trumpet notes
have cradled the world in blue for weeks
but today they cry like anarchic goats

pale as the sky bleached in haze overhead.
Babies keep whining in the long line of prams
from plaza to supermarket, impatient to consume.

Frank pays attention for the first time although
the queue has stood, undiminished, for years
just as the FTSE trampolining the pound

is, for some, a reason to live and, for others,
hidden as the rage of commuters on the bypass
or a life-support machine's final squeak.

In the hospital, Frank's baby's breath blew out
like the cherry blossom crash-landing around
the kerbs and drains, raised briefly with every

loitering hope and passing bus. The pram babies
linger like cappuccino froth or white candles waiting
to be lit on windowsills in favour of an unclear cause

while televisions drone on regardless. The trumpet
bleats. The reason for a note remains mysterious
until the next and then the next, just as commuters

beat out progress by traffic lights. The system
functions. The operation was successful for a time.
Her eyes opened, blue, for a moment blinked

and shut. The eighth day. He hears it is good
that tills keep clinking, that each day bears
its fair share of crashes, that disappointment

and music are made possible only by love.
The trumpet croaks a flat minim and Frank says,
'I tried I tried everything but nothing worked.'

Scottish Sonnet Ending in American

'We do not speak like Petrarch or wear a hat like Spenser
and it is not fourteen lines.'
                    — BILLY COLLINS from *American Sonnet*

I enter to the iambic whimpering
of cheerleaders at the Presbyterian Guild—
half-Calvinist, half-Muppet—and when expelled,
I ride a yellow cab to the *Shattered Wing*
where super-size-me drams are conjuring
nonce forms and shapeless beasts, which stagger wild
down yellow brick wynds from Wick to Cumbernauld,
one foot short of a rhythmic swing.

I beg them to conform, to recreate
the tartan utopia of Brigadoon
in my devolved, not quite united, state.

But then I goof like Bush or wear a hat
like Wayne. Or quit a sonnet on line thirteen

Fallen Villages of the North

Given the unreliable climate on the moors,
Longhorsley's priest supplies intercession
for pineapple experiments at Pauperhaugh
and genetically modified okra in Cockle Park.

Although he is diminutive in height
his giant thumbs drum up post-lapsarian boredom
long before the drone of cauliflower florets
ripens to a ceremonial trumpeting

at fairground season: time for merry-go-rounds
to recycle appearances, for technology to calculate
the caterpillar train's freight capacity
during its climactic, right-angled nosedive.

The rain runs amok with a chemical stink.
Cabbage allotments between rival chair-o-planes
raise leaves to heaven, green umbrellas
punctured in the heart of hail-bitten earth.

The old-timers still believe in growth
by steady grace, though most are stunted,
which keeps in mind their need for God, in love,
to sling thunderclouds above evil

Shilbottle's battered crèpe stall awnings,
to give hurricanes the run of its skyscraping
big wheel. Bananas, force-fed ethylene, sweat
carbon dioxide, the priest's *basso profundo* shakes

coconuts from the shy, 'And did those feet . . .'
through sunburn, sandblast and snowstorm,
while all-weather saviours drop like shells
in triumph to the leaky inflatable slide.

Moving On

The tall haystacks are great sugar mounds
These are the fairies' camping grounds
                    —JOHN ASHBERY, AGED 8

When I first encountered imagination in Bronco's barn,
cornstalk in my mouth and liquorice melting in my pocket,
I could tell my career as a poet was over.
How can one follow such a couplet, except with
another couplet? I see it now in my friends' marriages
dividing every day into further failures, which continue
to multiply. When Liz Taylor had married seven times—
a sonnet!—you'd think that would have been the perfect
time to stop, but the usual imagined future egged her on.
Take the pea-pod half I launched into the pond last year,
which washed up on a deserted shore and soon became
part of the island scenery, a boat-shaped hold-all
cramming sunlight and breadfruit among my sweaty
T-shirts and trainers. Every day, I press
a coconut shell to my lips and reflect on whether rescue
is desirable. Rescue by fairies perhaps! Now where did
that come from, and where did they go?

Scotlands

Just when we think we have arrived, the coach jolts forward
from the Sorley Maclean Appreciation Society Picnic,

which once had been the terminus on this excursion
through healthy weeds, peat bogs, and everlasting rain.

Although we still hear mouth music in the distance,
the accent is American, the language a kind of English

and the entire population is queuing round the clock
for pizza, chicken vindaloo, and deep-fried Mars Bar.

At six degrees, it's the warmest day in Falkirk this year,
but the coach shoots past for the Museum of Scotland

and a quick dose of reality—our miserable record of defeats
in battle against ourselves. When we emerge,

Edinburgh has disappeared, and a choir of Tartan Tories
improvises *God Save The Queen* on Culloden Field

while we photograph the grass. 'Much too green,'
someone says, which induces a predictable backlash

from the ecumenical contingent. Everyone now feels
discriminated against and half the passengers board

a ferry to Nova Scotia. We hear many have drowned
by the time we reach Glasgow's suburban sprawl

and there is bitterness, bitterness against those who left,
bitterness at the speedbumps, bitterness that the Scots

Dictionary compiler has bonded with the monoglot
tour guide, bitterness at being left behind, perhaps to die

in these plush leather seats, bitterness at the angle
we approach the Sacred Cows statuette, but nevertheless

enchantment at the world beyond the windows—on one side
a row of builders' bums and flash women, and on the other

a child crouched by the bonnie bonnie banks of Loch Lomond,
blowing dandelion clocks, which fan out on a tail wind's

whistle-stop tour of common ground, each fibre waiting for
the sudden drop, for a patch of earth in which to root itself.

Nuclear Submarines

One day they will surely betray me.
For now, they seem content to drowse

resolutely without wit or purpose
like autistic sharks ballooning

through seaweed, rock and sand
of fish cities deep in blackout.

While I'm trying to trust, one breaks
the Gareloch's surface and fixes

its stunned gaze on the mirrored sky.
Things are as they should be—

the clouds, the flotsam, the stranger
peering from the shore with my face.

The second it drops, I no longer exist.
It has no memory, no plans.

The water rises, the sky falls,
and I am as blue is to the fish.

Everyone Will Go Crazy

The number ten to Morningside tailgates a cyclist.
'Me next, me next!' Obese kids bicker over possession
of the console and, outside, drunks in kilts pelt

Poles with cabbage from a restaurant wheelie bin.
The best wee country, where arms flap and buses
whistle by. If the driver picks up the Poles

fifty yards past the stop, everyone will go crazy.
We provide uncertain guidelines in every language.
Brian craves the simplicity of Space Invaders,

the bleep of a Casio VL-Tone, even switching off
is so complex these days. The psychiatric hospital,
invisible from the road, prioritises social inclusion.

'It's my turn, you bastard!' *We treasure customers
with overwhelming indifference.* The cyclist wobbles,
the opposite of cabbage—such a solid vegetable,

fat as a bus honk—and, on the radio, a Wal-Mart
lackey raves, 'Our mission is to save people
from money.' *In think tanks we fabricate personal*

airspace. With a day pass from the low-risk ward
Brian plots to annex Buckingham Palace and dictate
legislation on body shape conformity. He craves lack

of choice on the shelves. *The small print reflects
an ethos of multinational lip-service.* Independence
within Europe. A massive cabbage blasts the cyclist

into orbit, while Poles dive for cover, kids click
the console frantically, 'You *noob!*' and Brian says,
'They really ought to speak English if they live here.'

The Loser

He lost with a symbolic victory secured.
Deep in the forest, acolytes resurrected him
from dying leaves, crisp, and with a throat of fire,
but no heat, no light, only autumn lit the eyes,
his arms olive, backside birch, ponytail willow,
connected by shade, congealed in smirr, eschewing
the crutch of twig or bone. He mounted his plinth
and raised a fist of triumphant pine.

The winds could have blown. Instead they beat out
terms of supremacy behind closed doors, hailed deadlock
as democracy and flung a nailed-down table
through the triple glazing as evidence of purpose,
catalyst for a national year of rain, and so on
towards a mulch kingdom, mosquito hatchery.
His opponents wasted time waving matches at the weather.
He dripped, became unrecognisable and in control.

While the Moonies are Taking Over Uruguay

While the Moonies are taking over Uruguay,
I find time to skin these *peperoni*,
grilled but resistant to peeling.

Is God to blame when his chosen people
scribble battle-plans and draft rackets
in his name? Does he need

Uruguay? The hotels fall into Moonie hands,
then the corporate bodies. Bids begin
for Catholic mass.

Pepper juice squirts on my wrists, sticky
like blueberry grappa. I regret
trying this recipe.

The Montevideo football stadiums host
communal weddings. Thousands
of strangers queue in twos

like Fiats boxed in the rush-hour crawl,
and my guests will be late. *Che peccato!*
I chop fennel into strips.

By Torino's *Porta Nuova* train station,
the Jehovah's Witnesses stalk me
with magazines, and talk

peace. The Mormons attack *Via Garibaldi*,
suits and ties in the summer heat
and still they don't sweat.

Is it a miracle? Next to them, Africans
hawk cheap sunglasses with fake
UVA protection,

but what Italian doesn't yet own a pair?
Only the Mormons do without,
wide-eyed and blinkered.

The garlic sizzles. I add onion. The Moonies
plant a flag in an empty field, somewhere
near Fray Bentos.

I am left with my small concerns; the time
to add the rosemary, the freshly
snapped corkscrew.

Tonight, if the *peperoni* will, we may
taste God among us. And later,
there shall be *tiramisù*.

Berlusconi and the National Grid

Berlusconi prayed daily for extra channels.

God replied with lightning,
short-circuited the National Grid for hours.

'That's the nature of power,' old men
mumbled to their empty espresso cups—
'Press the right switches
and everyone stops watching.'

Berlusconi summoned Milan's darkness,
the fascist architecture of the railway station,
a third-class compartment to Eboli
for communists and illegals.

'Forza Italia!' he cheered
and when no one answered
declared a state of paranoia.

Lights snapped back in unison.
He blamed the power-cut on a tree that fell
somewhere in Switzerland.

In Italy, he promised, trees will be taught
not to lean at inconvenient angles.

Shopping List

... baked beans, cauliflower, a helicopter
blinks across the sky. That's all it takes to grab
a piece of him these days, light up
and he'll plead for you, for onions,
radishes, you name it. Somewhere between
a casual one-night stand and sex
among cigarettes, polo mints, aubergines,
casualties, there is room
for communication, one may hope. No doubt
it could mean less than coffee grains, bread
for toasting, as she showers him
from her skin and he contemplates the layout
of the supermarket, haggis, four cheese
pizza, sauerkraut, his breath
stale as morning, the dull
streetlamp beyond the window capturing the free
range eggs, cod in batter,
toothpaste, false mood, and when
she emerges from an age
in the bathroom, her hair shampooed
and her body wrapped in raw
prawns, lasagne, an old towel, he realises
she is young and classy, almost
a trophy, and his words tumble out, Can we cling
film, greaseproof paper, silver foil, see
each other? but these items
are scored off the list.

Patenting The

After The the Company Ltd patented definite
article and hired headless mannequin
to enforce non-specificity, longing
in high streets, as statistics proved,
was for clarity. 'Rotate for us head
of mannequin on plate that we might
rate all sides!' roared shoppers from
roundabouts now identical to town
squares. The the Company Ltd estimated
insufficient evidence of traffic casualty
increase and applauded initiative
of acolyte badgewearers who downloaded
mall musak ring-tones and guillotined
themselves in sympathy. 'Bring us Sun!
Bring us exclusive offer, please! Bring us
Queen!' bawled shoppers, flitting between
movie, band and sovereign, but when
I, or fluid identity bearing my pronoun,
googled myself and found only evidence
of non-existence, I was decreed too
disappointingly subjective. They spun me
and I am spinning still, seeking truth,
but neither mannequin nor unsynchronised
shoppers are clear on which truth to deny me.

Bananas

With each edition of today's *Evening News*,
a free banana. And no, this is not a wind-up
or some poetic artifice at work on your
subconscious—the banana means nothing
other than itself. You can read the news,
banana in hand, and with each mouthful,
the page will soften its focus until only
the horoscope feels like harder copy
than the banana's flesh. If you decide,
on the basis of today's experiment,
that tomorrow's banana cannot come
quick enough, the early editions will carry
a free DVD of a Hollywood movie no one
has never seen. An imaginary banana
will pop up around the one-hour mark.
If you try a banana once, you can't stop.

Scotland

after Alastair Reid

It was a day common in this corner of the planet,
when daffodils bent double in sleet and wind,
and black umbrellas shattered in the hand.
Spring lay buried in dirt. Greyness entered
the skin. I pressed through empty Sabbath streets—
the nation was shopping in the malls, or choosing
Swedish furniture to compensate for the woodchip
on its walls. I found a Starbucks and a woman
of uncommon beauty behind the counter.
'What a morning!' I cried. 'Why not try an extra shot
of espresso?' she replied. 'It's just the day for it.'
Her smile brightened the hour and meant
Now pay for it, and pay for it, and pay for it.

How New York You Are

How New York you are, Edinburgh, crammed to your turrets with
    legends of cultural centrality
you still believe in. From a bed-sit in Gorgie Road, Gordon, Ralph
    and Bill fantasise about
dragging the most vital and mimetically-daring creative writing
    students of the millennium
over to Bill's lawnmower palace for a reading. Gordon wants lots of
    attractive women, 'It's the 20th century!'
he insists at 2.47 p.m. on 22 August 2007, but Ralph the promoter
    reckons females and even gays
are too damn powerful, although he believes in forgiveness and
    equality up to a point.
Yes, there will be an anthology, yes, it will feature himself, yes,
    the front cover will be bagpipes
and yes, he will hold a launch packed with Scottish semi-finalists
    from *Britain's Got Talent*
and impenetrable performance artists discovered on the world's
    most vandalised park bench,
and yes, Bill can read a few, the one with a line for each step up
    the Scott Monument,
the one about the lost youth of Cockburn Street, but not the one
    about the bitter author
he once saw on television, however chilling. 'How New York you
    are, Edinburgh!' Gordon interjects,
as Beth the painter drops in from another day replicating with oil
    the dogshit in Saughton Park,
and everyone suddenly feels part of something much bigger than
    themselves, as if on the brink
of placing something in the *East Lothian Review* at the ninety-fourth
    attempt in two years
after a rejection slip signed personally with the editor's initials in
    blue biro

gave them a stab of hope last week, but Beth is high and stinking
      and wants a slice
of Bill's *Deep Pan* Ham and Mushroom pizza, which 'just goes to
      prove my point,' says Ralph.
Gordon tells how he's starting an online literary magazine for poems
      no one else wants to read,
how he's so far been flooded with submissions, enough for three
      issues on much-mourned aunts.
If only he could hook up with local film directors and cutting-edge
      impresarios of anything,
he's sure something would come of it. 'They all go to London,'
      he says. 'They come back
after meeting Dame Judi Dench and Paris Hilton at some awful party
      and want *my* sympathy,'
at which point Bill's face collapses into what's left of his pizza and
      no one knows whether
he's drunk, asleep, or dead, or whether he's just being New York in
      that knowing way
he has when pursuing art and Ralph leaves and Gordon leaves and
      Beth grabs a final slice and leaves.

The Look

Inside the café window I slither past, anxious
at the threat of rain, a woman stares into her teacup
where a miniature nude thrashes among the leaves.
Our one-way connection fizzles out and sixty watts
of blown bulb blacken the telescope's view
of the boudoir where Madame beds down
in darkness with a negligee and iPod. Recorded
music these days is so realistic I can almost
see it—the new Rihanna single, for example:
a woodlouse entering a crack in the compost heap.
Each weekday, my practised gaze falls on young
mothers wielding pushchairs like lawnmowers
through city parks, leaving great lines of orderliness
and pressed flowers in their wake, and I count
how many children I might have fathered
if fatherhood could be accomplished by a glance.
No one has seen God the Father, but he must keep
tabs on me if either of us continues to exist. What of
existence? I'd prefer not to witness the nude's desperate
stretch for the cup's rim, unable to haul himself
over the edge of a precipice he believes imaginary
and I hear the café has introduced a dishwasher.

Hot Shit

Like a microphone
the HP sauce bottle
sticks to his lips.

A commis chef venerates
the white blaze of his throat,
his offering to the sewer rat.

Pigs head-butt the exit.
When the door creaks open
the pigs stay put.

In dumb misfortune
a one-armed-bandit blinks.
Speech! Speech! the cabbage cries.

A pan spits
applause for his scatty eloquence,
his joke about rattling fire.

Women he swears
he never slept with rise
from a circle of hollow birthday cakes.

Slimming

Slim-hipped, they said, and draped her in a dress
of pink velvet. *So cute.* She tried to eat
but she was skin on bone, and butterfat
made her sick. *An angel full of grace,*
empty of meat. When she began to trace
her figure on a wooden spoon, they thought
grease supplements might raise her weight
and ordered Quarter Pounders to excess.

Their sterile house stank like a burger bar
for years. She shrank further: *a twig, a wire,*
a scrape of nail, as if she couldn't bear
to share a table with the world's desire
for growth. Soon only a motion would declare
her presence: *heaven's breath*, inhale, expire.

Girl Playing Sudoku on the Seven-Fifteen

I sit down opposite. She doesn't blink
or cough, her pencil-scratch the only noise
beyond the train's dull chitchat. Teenage boys
slouch up the centre-aisle, unleash the stink
of *Lynx*. She keeps on scrawling to the brink
of suffocation. I admire her poise,
open windows, plumb my brain for ploys
to start a conversation. I can't think.

Our eyes squint out of sync. Although I stare,
I don't dare interrupt her concentration
and when she finally completes the square
I focus on the floor. One hesitation
begins a chain. I set up solitaire.
The train heaves on, already past my station.

Homes of the Future Exhibition

Tonight, the future apes the present
in tan and amber naugahyde, sparks debate
on whether tigers best accessorise a wall
or floor, on whether your most recent wife
outclasses the taxidermy demonstrator
with a degree in feng shui. 'A job must lead
to something,' your wife says, as ever,
definite but lacking clarity, and you can't
fathom the attraction. You're bowled over by
the pleathers collection and place deposits
on kitchens with fast-track toasters. Here's how
your job has shaped you: a stuffed feline tongue,
a vacuum cleaner fat with dust, starved
always, but without needs. Your wife's skin
is corporate, a fresh line in surgically applied
spandex, smooth as velour. You touch it
tenderly from time to time, but she feels
nothing and you may as well be abstract,
you may as well strike matches in a corner
until the rafters blaze. If nothing catches,
this version of time will continue to darken
the dinosaur museum, featuring the assembled
cast of some B-movie, where you're the tour guide
and can't pronounce the simplest of names.

In the Last Few Seconds

In a smudge of tail-lights you watch your soul go,
then you spin round corners you would have taken
slow before you gulped back the rum. The bottle
     rocks on the backseat.

When a soul slips off, does it shed its body
and the drink that drives it? Or keep guard over
falling debris? Nights like this drop like voices,
     warning that all roads

end in vapour; nothing turns blank so gently
as a hairpin bend on a high cliff. Headlights
catch the grassy verge where you lose control, rouse
     breakers like sparklers

from the wind-scrubbed inlet. The impact crushes
bones to powder, slows up the sinking. Husks of
crumpled metal, covered in rust and seaweed,
     smear at the bottom.

You expect a flashback, a potted bio
of divorce and automobile replacement—
how one breakage led to another—film noir
     bleaching the blackness,

but instead stars blister across the sunroof.
Cracks appear. You wait for the tunnel sponged in
light from some new world. But the car splits water,
     floats in its shadow.

Benediction
for Alexander Hutchison

The festival officials haul the chipped stone Virgin
from the oversize cathedral, furnish her with swimwear,

truck her through town in a luminous pink catafalque,
Madonna of Candyfloss and Sugar-Plum, fashioned by

Gucci bikini, geologic surgery, and bottle-blonde wig
as Paris Hilton look-a-like, fist raised, a fallen saint.

Crowds line the streets to hail her as a C-list celebrity,
offspring of the *Hello* back issue currently smothering

a tramp's benched head. Her eyelids shut,
open, and lava-hot tears steam towards the crowd.

The officials, from their high terrace, seize
the photo opportunity, kneel, catch the sulphurous whiff

of miracle, and bless the harvest swaying in the fields.
The townspeople burn and howl for forgiveness.

Hospital

Third left in the terminal zone—
ignore the fluorescent light
insistent as a flatline tone.
Hug therapies are on the right.

Ignore the fluorescent light.
Stretch out where butchery takes place.
Hug therapies are on the right
with a professional embrace.

Stretch out where butchery take place
on the body's artful smorgasbord.
With a professional embrace
the surgeons work on being adored.

On the body's artful smorgasbord,
florid designer-scars are kissed.
The surgeons work on being adored
by the glum basement anaesthetist.

Florid designer-scars are kissed.
Love letters ignite unread
by the glum basement anaesthetist
who tests the eyelids of the dead.

Love letters ignite unread.
A matron laps at cheap rosé.
Who tests the eyelids of the dead?
The anaesthetist has slept away.

A matron laps at cheap rosé,
insistent as a flatline tone.
The anaesthetist has slept away—
third left in the terminal zone.

Visiting Hour

A parrot enters, perhaps a cockatoo,
disguised as his daughter.

Tennis on television.
She flutters for the off-switch.

The hawks fuss with their uniforms
until the signal to swoop.

From the blank screen, his eyes stare
at the scat of themselves.

She hovers, even though
she is not a hawk.

Her beak nuzzles his hair.
She will drop him to her squealing nest.

A young dove, wrapped up
in his own mythology, affirms a pulse.

The freshly perfumed hawks
beat out their applause.

Advice from the Lion Tamer to the Poetry Critic

1. Never go into the cage
   without knowing
   what kind of day the poem is having.

2. You must approach the poem
   with the aim of having
   the poem approach you.

3. You've got to get inside
   the poem's skull.

4. Ask first—
   'Is now a good time to meet?'

5. When poems leap through hoops of fire
   it must not appear
   that you helped them do it.

6. Read the poem's
   behaviour.

7. Quiet poems need subtler handling
   than roaring ones,
   but all poems are in thrall
   to their own voices.

8. To survive, learn to value
   your instinct.

9. The poem snarls
   if you look for thanks.

10. The poem is *never* tame.

11. You need to know
    when to get out of the cage.

12 A display of temper leads
    to an early grave.

Some lines, phrases sourced from *Lion Taming* (Sourcebooks, Illinois 2004) by Steven L. Katz, used with the author's permission.

A Creative Writing Tutor Addresses his Star Pupil

Now you must write a sestina that spawns
a killer line unexpectedly cut
short
to assert freedom from the chains of form,
yet show ease with it. Above all, you must
end a line with the words 'John Ashbery' —

that's the benchmark of style. 'John Ashbery!'
The mere citation of his oeuvre spawns
a catholic, poetic hush. You must
speak it with reverence. Words should be cut
until distilled right-brain processes form
in varied registers. Poems should be short

enough to run the average reader's short
attention span - he knows John Ashbery
but only the first lines. John wrote in form
initially, and some say his work spawns
most sonnets written now. Some want to cut
him from the canon, tsk tsk, so you must

read *Flow Chart* at least once a month, you must
stumble across meaning the way a short-
circuit in a grid trips to a perfect cut
in light — a metaphor John Ashbery
would die for, I'd like to think. My verse spawns
the seed of future Ashbery, a form

of testament. When I type on top form
I tap out metre. That is one skill you must
cultivate. You'll see that trochees spawn
a cultural abyss after a short-
lived flirtation. Like John Ashbery,
you'll have nightmares in anapaests until you cut

your counting fingers off. To make the cut
of poets-found-in-schoolbooks, do not conform,
and try this iambic prayer: 'John Ashbery!
John Ashbery!' a mantra that you must
repeat until the sounds fall quick and short
as one sound falls. A true teacher spawns

countless John Ashberys. Today you must
form yourself from your Maker's voice. No short
cut exists, my pupil, my eager spawn.

The Kingdom

God's knock is soft as pumpkin pie, not the rap
I thought I'd have to take, or the oddly undersize
boot of a superpower. I open up. He leads me out
through the cardboard arch where celebrities scramble
for *McDonalds* off-cuts in the border ditch
and talk of Michelangelo with personal coaches.
Heavenly choirs ironize Marilyn Manson, their hymns
jazz up Calvin, the popes queue like schoolboys
to plink on the honky-tonk piano. No one gives a fuck about
the Da Vinci code and despite protests from the Governor
of California, the table wine is always French.

Married Life in the Nineties

DERRIDA

*'My most resolute opponents believe that I am too visible, that I am a little
too alive, that my name echoes too much in the texts which they nevertheless
claim to be inaccessible.'*
— JACQUES DERRIDA

You fielded questions with quotes from Derrida
and blamed Miss Garlick's Pop Literature course
for some inner trauma you couldn't bear to name,
left, like most things, muzzled and obvious.

Rottweilers prowled in swing parks, cleared
gangs from the night, kids from the day.
I ran in fear while you threw them liver-chunks,
confirming your unilateral decision

to go vegetarian; this was how your brain worked —
incomprehensible explosions without admission
of responsibility. I was like a thought you once had
and soon an injury friends kept enquiring after.

True, we had favourite restaurants where muzak
reminded us of similar muzak, where waiters
brought cider with your curry before you asked
and you memorised the menus through every course.

How Derrida the menus were! He was everywhere,
in your hair, in my hair loss, in every solid the air
squashed around, but by the time I made the effort
to check him out, you had moved onto Wim Wenders

and film theory. I knew his soundtracks off by heart.

Spliced and Fading Out

'If you play this stuff backwards, it says, 'This sucks !"
— Butthead

I remember the queen scowling from coins,
Love is All Around in personal stereo multiplying
from a shop window's television stack.

My band shared a studio with Wet Wet Wet
and set Radio Scotland briefly alight, spliced
to an enigmatic Kronos Quartet fade-out

I preserved on cassette. Strangers shouted
'Wazzuuup!' to strangers. By osmosis, fat
became the new ordinary. Soon 'real' was

the opposite of 'thin', 'fuck you' a synonym
for 'caring Conservatism'. We rarely conversed.
I practised Beavis and Butthead impressions

on the subway. You preferred to hang around
Gaelic hubs. A magic tree laced your neck
in place of a crucifix men couldn't help kissing.

You emblazoned T-shirts with CAUTION which,
eventually, failed to ignite. I determined
to ignore the shine of the times, the slobbery

slope to the waif look and Gigapet, and held out
for whatever was due beyond Windows 95 —
a rash of holidays in separate cathedral cities.

I wrote songs about how I almost loved you
and appointed other men to sing them.
Sometimes you tra-la'd them at peace rallies

where you met a chap who believed porridge
could break the capitalist cereal industry.
His record collection was solid Dylan.

You felt called to save him from his struggle
with continental lager—leaving me, I presumed,
either self-sufficient or without hope.

The Deconstruction Industry

Late Sunday afternoon, a disused church
is demolished to accommodate
splashdown crossroads and tramline fragments.

Tomorrow, regular pedestrians will ask,
'What used to be there?'

Traffic cones police the abyss,
battle embarrassment
in amber hats.

Muscled men swing wrecking balls
between billboards and referents.

Restored in fibreglass, the national ruin
dwarfs the shorn tenements.

Aftershaves cultivate the attitude
of pneumatic drills.

Three teenagers confess to a CCTV camera
that they expect nothing but hope
for whatever's left over.

Hangover Hotel

He hears the bellhop humming in the lobby—
the theme from *Van der Valk*—and minutes later,
the same tune drifts from speakers hidden
behind papier-mâché trees, blasted, it seems,
with a synthetic form of Dutch Elm disease.

The air is like breath distilled and bottled
from a Sunday dawn. He refills his glass
and finds a small, square patch of disco
where trained apes chant steps and monitor
arm movements of the awkward men,

where women dab approved scents in unison,
branded, blurbed and sponsored by the sisters
from Our Lady of Perpetual Meltdown, desirable
in their unaffordability. A recess off the superloo
doubles as the Chapel of Reflection and offers

full communion with a PradaGirl or BabeNextDoor.
He slips a coin into a slot and neither body
judders out. The attendant shakes his head,
he speaks only Latin, and the cloakroom staff
spin yarns in dead dialect, all of them claiming

residency of some in-between state where
tonal registers bleep incompatibly, but now
the speed dating has begun and he is late
to table, too late for the bottle blondes, although
apocalyptic bingo-callers still wait in hope.

There is a bar to be drunk dry and once
everything is past recall, to be drunk again,
and chat-up lines to mouth from tongue
to tongue in thirty-second intervals until
everyone has passed out or passed

away. At the Hangover Hotel, transience
is the new rock'n'roll, the same old story
no one remembers for long, no matter
how many mini-bars he empties
or rooms he trashes—it's never enough,

the amenities are limitless. He must sample
the slime Jacuzzi, the talcum cocaine,
and here's another human torch streaking
from reception with an anguished grin, glass
in hand, careful not to spill even a drop.

Edinburgh in Summer

Edinburgh rouses its broad avenues,
the diplomatic nous of its dead volcano.
It grants citizenship to lawnmowers,
tolerates wielders of bloody scythes.

Neighbours lock tongues to avoid
confrontation. Men with pointy beards
seal themselves in toilet cubicles
and cultivate philosophies of death.

Such rainfall that unemployed arsonists
surrender their matches. Local columns
no longer crinkle by violet light.
Smoke hibernates in a polyester blouse.

Only the blue-rinsed dames pack
handbags with rocks and pin
umbrella spokes to the eyes of strangers
who lean into their comfort zone.

Jacko Holed Up In Blackfriars Street B and B?

The day after he disappears, rumours cruise the boudoirs and dens
of Aberdeen. The offshore oilmen use up their annual leave
and strain their eyes for a sighting. Look-a-likes flock
to the city, best known for its granite façade,
its sightless glare. Mask-makers and dance instructors
declare an unexpected boom, which takes their minds off the rising
price of flounder and the small hole widening at
the bottom of the North Sea. The oil-wives, two weeks on

Local Woman's Third-Cousin's Nephew Foils Saddam's Army

two weeks off, had sprinkled their suburban lawns
until the hosepipe ban. They stand by their taps and wait
for the wind to change, the clouds to collide. Against all predictions

Bosnian Clash Shock To North-East Economy

hail and fog quench the Indian summer, and Jackson
boogies down Union Street unhindered, spotted only
by a sharp-eyed drunk outside the shopping centre
around 3am. This city is best left to the gust
of self-induced bluster. 'Who cares about the black

Nationalist Councillor Apologises For England Oil Slur

bastard? I lived through two world wars!' —
some old fascist in the pension queue makes
his logical connections. The wives pump up the hosepipes again
now that the grass is wet, now that the husbands
are counting the days back to work. This city is best seen at night
next to a traffic light. He sings 'Billie Jean' by the maritime museum
to a group of adolescents who mistake him
for Ali G and ask him to cadge them

[44]

Aberdeen Fishmonger Blames Rwanda Bloodbath For Doomed Love

twelve cans of Tennant's lager. Rumour has it that when the oil
drains away, town planners will dredge up a new Aberdeen
in Eastern Mauritania, with a bar and goldfish pond
ninety miles down a sand-track. The wives forecast gales
as helicopters rock their men to the next fortnight's

University Professor Spots Jackson Leaving Dyce Airport

relief. Pressmen summon headlines, silhouettes, blurred outlines,
unreliable witnesses, and conjure the evening's final run.
Jackson turns up next morning, asleep in a public toilet cubicle
near Connecticut, best experienced as an act of imagination.
Some say the attendant's maternal great-grandfather may have swiped
a rowie from a bakery on the North Sea coast.

My Dentist, Aniela

My Polish dentist, Aniela, may condescend
to drill NHS patients, but not as a concession
to the old values. Wives would have been good
for the Popes, she opines, and communism
was a mug's game. Does she remember
Jan Tomaszewski's heroic saves against England
in 1974? No, she was *unborn*. She dates
a Cowdenbeath supporter. Casually. Everything
she does is casual. She fills a needle. Her breasts
bunch into my arm as she bends to explore
my gums, a cultural boob—taboo, I suppose,
and some people fear touch and pay
not to see her, preferring the stench of Mr McPhee's
private sector armpits, the pointless exclusivity
and designer décor at the Upper Crust branch—
aluminium chairs so nineties that any day now
they will be retro-chic. She leans further in,
asks if there is any sensation, and perhaps
too vehemently, I issue denials. When it comes
to extraction, she conceals her technology
between lethal fingertips, grip enough to snap
a chicken's neck with one twist. She raises
a bloody bone in triumph and handkerchiefs it
dry. When she draws her eyes level,
travels my bottom lip with her thumb nail,
and asks again, I tell her I never felt a thing.

Breaking the Hoodoo

So here we are again, as the Rovers attempt
to break a twenty-year hoodoo at Stenhousemuir
before a crowd of near fifty and a pack of dogs
that yowl at every foul throw-in. A team of jokers
and Bovril drinkers. One of them is blind and waves
his white stick at what appears to be the ball,
but it's a head trundling through the centre circle's
scuff and mud. The referee's attention wanders
for a second and that's what happens! Tubby McHugh
gets off with a booking, the linesman saw a sword
flashing through the air from the corner of his eye.
And the forwards! Yesterday, they took their first lesson
in keepie-up. No joke. Someone please introduce them
to hand-ball, the offside rule, the direct approach.
Nutmegged again! Stenhousemuir attack, the dogs
snore. Rovers are 2–0 down, and on the team stretcher
the chairman and his trophy wife are dry fucking
in their Barcelona tracksuits. Look away! Because
two own goals in two minutes have evened the score,
and Jinxy limps on with five minutes left. He creaks
down the wing, that's fifty-eight years in the top flight,
yet some say he died after his third stroke, OK then,
a corpse, but he still carves through the outstretched legs
and flying rugby tackles of the Stenhousemuir defence.
The referee clamps a whistle to his mouth, the dogs
gargle loudly. Only the goalkeeper stands between Jinxy
and the widening goalmouth, the net also stretching out
until it covers the nation in cross-stitched shadow
and dwarfs the players, the pitch, the hissing cats
at the corner flag, the Saltires waving from the pie stall.
The goalkeeper is staring wildly at his broken stopwatch
as every last shot in the game comes steaming in.

Sevenling (Elizabeth had II)

Elizabeth had II moulded on the post boxes.
She was the first of Scotland and the UK. My uncles
posted three matches and burned a box away.

The nineteenth century acts defined English
as a language and Scots a dialect. Gaelic was
a silence; the cane stroked it out the schools.

Language dies from imprecision. Numbers adapt.

Plastic Cork

Some things don't belong together, like 'plastic'
and 'cork'; or you, me and a long evening in
after the informal split, with the lamb joint
still bloody in the oven and the stars
smudging the haar outside the window.

Before we know it, the long gap between 'semi'
and 'naked' is being bridged
and meaningless acts are taking place
beneath the table. Afterwards you switch the TV off—
a documentary on tourism you'd watched
with half an eye. You take your coat,
walk out into the fog, as if 'something'
and 'nothing' were all part of the same thing.

Sky Blue

In a polo shirt and sky blue boots I walk
in the wake of self-aware travel diarists
and potential blindness. The sun is so bright
it's impossible to miss anything, and so
the roadside Oracle of Invisible Being
gets my full attention. I have a sky blue heart,
it tells me and also that from today Paris
is the capital of Poland. It's hard not to feel
I'm being taken for a ride. Every ten minutes
a tiny Boeing 757 floats from one cloud
to another and back again. I always look,
then look down at the boots, reassuringly
sky blue on the gravel between nettles
and pockets of darkness. Beyond both,
poppies stretch for miles, each stem tilting
an identical face to the sun, not knowing
or caring if anyone focuses in. And yes,
I am equally puzzling to myself, equally
apparent in my sky blue boots, tilting now to
this flower, now this one, this one, that one.

The Preacher's Ear

They are building flats for the widowed poor along my street.
They rattle and drill through the day.

I pitch a deep sermon to the flock, who nod, and knit
their quiet eventide away.

Someone wolf-whistles to a young nun. My head sings with it at night,
with thin bells the wind hammers near, with prayers left to lapse,

with church steeples struck by lightning
and then collapsed.

They are building for the lonely dying. They are building
silent, terracotta corridors

and walls without shade. Someone bumps down a Bible
in every room. They slam the drawers,

clang the scaffolding. They know I hear them. I pitch
a shallow sermon to myself, and nod, the way

I often nod at anything. They are building lifts
that roar between floors, and halfway

between, start falling. Someone slaps putty on a widening rift.
They expect my application any day, the first jangling of the keys.

I pitch an evangelical sermon to the breeze. They are installing chains
and zimmer frames and chopping up the trees.

Let these signs mark where the pandemonium ends.
If angels pitch on my behalf, I can't hear them.

Holiday at the New Butlins

Blind forty, it's Christmas in July, the bingo-caller
suits her Santa hat, two slim ladies wait for eighty-eight,
will wait until the pantomime reindeer from Huddersfield
samba to Slade, anachronistic Yorkshire camouflaged
as family entertainment, *your place or mine, sixty-nine*,
lager flattening in my glass, a drink for the elves in case
their boss fails to show, *dearie me, number three*, my kid makes
a fake claim, the spotlight pirouettes around her anguished
mother's exit, that trim backside almost liturgical,
did you score, twenty-four, did you score? I answer for her
in negative, too loud, for me the fattened battery
bird squawks undying contempt, I love you, *flea in heaven,
thirty-seven*, I love you echoes round the hall, fades to
a fairy light, then a useless *fourteen, Valentine's Day.*

Glory Box
for Anne

For his forty-third birthday party he blows up
an adult bouncy castle and entertains his guests
with old trip hop covers on acoustic guitar,

Give me a reason to love you . . . An hour later
we make our excuses. Love is difficult enough
in normal circumstances but at the intersection

of theology and real life, where the angel Barbie
scours the magazine gossip, *Why I Scrubbed
my Face with Brillo Pads*, the hermeneutic circle

in word and sacrament steeling itself at this
latest assault on established doctrine, we find
half an afternoon to reconnect romantically

in a chic Italian snug before the question must
again be asked, *Why?* If tools for flagellation
weren't available, the woman had to make do

with whatever was lying around, I suggest,
but you're more impressed with the marinade
firing up the olives, and the wine, house,

but bloody fantastic. The church secretary
wants a raise and to know whether Jesus died
to forgive sin or reveal it already forgiven

as the last nail was hammered in, and is shocked
to know this was a source of nineteenth century
internal strife, *I've been a temptress too long*

still fogging up my head like a disputed text—
two minutes on the bouncy castle, a lifetime
with you, not long enough, theologically speaking.

The Scuffle

That shape in the garden—how could it not
have been metaphorical? A fox attacked a teabag
on my frozen lawn. I threw it a mould
of sandwich, left myself famished
and the fridge empty, ideal conditions
for a magnum opus. I published a universal
moral code days later. The idea that needs
connect, including imaginary ones, was the root
of my system: the twinning of hunger
in the garden and the satisfaction
I dreamed I'd feel. My code inspired
the movie of an untranslatable lyric, a shameless
get-rich-quick scheme approved by the latest
council report. Hollywood declared
an interest in the garden scuffle and, despite
adjustments, the screenplay's closing scenes
have clearly lost their focus, as endings should do
according to one school or another.

Lightning Source UK Ltd.
Milton Keynes UK
11 September 2010
159735UK00001B/8/P